BOLLINGEN SERIES LXX

THE KARIYE DJAMI

VOLUME 2 *of the publication*

of an archaeological project of

THE BYZANTINE INSTITUTE, INC.

PAUL A. UNDERWOOD

Rev. Joseph W. Bentha

THE KARIYE DJAMI

Volume 2   Plates 1–334

The Mosaics

BOLLINGEN SERIES LXX / PANTHEON BOOKS

THIS IS THE SECOND VOLUME OF A PUBLICATION
CONSTITUTING THE SEVENTIETH WORK IN BOLLINGEN SERIES
PUBLISHED BY BOLLINGEN FOUNDATION

Bollingen Foundation wishes to acknowledge with gratitude
the generous contribution of the Samuel H. Kress Foundation
toward the cost of the color plates for this volume.

Library of Congress Catalogue Card No. 65–10404

Manufactured in the United States of America
DESIGNED BY ANDOR BRAUN

Contents

List of Plates

Numbers in brackets are the numbers applied by the author to the mosaic subjects in the church. They correspond to the numbers appearing in red on the plans and sections and cited in brackets in the text and on the plates. Asterisks before plate numbers indicate plates printed in color.

GENERAL VIEWS

THE MOSAICS

ORNAMENTS

THE KARIYE DJAMI

PLATES

The Mosaics

The Kariye Djami. West façade

The Kariye Djami. View from the southeast

The Kariye Djami. View from the east

The nave. Looking east

The nave. Looking west

The nave. Looking north

The nave. Looking south

The nave. View into the dome from the northeast

The nave. View of the floor from the north

The outer narthex. Looking north

The outer narthex. Looking south

The outer narthex. The first, second, and third bays, looking northeast

The outer narthex. The third bay, looking southeast through the door to the inner narthex

The inner narthex. Looking north

The inner narthex. Looking south

The inner narthex. Looking southeast into the fourth bay

Christ Pantocrator

[1]

Christ Pantocrator. Detail

[1]

Christ Pantocrator. Detail: head

[I]

The Virgin Blachernitissa and angels

[2]

The Virgin Blachernitissa and angels. Detail: the Virgin

[2]

The Virgin Blachernitissa and angels. Detail: head of the Virgin

[2]

The Virgin Blachernitissa and angels. Detail: the Infant Christ

[2]

The Virgin Blachernitissa and angels. Detail: angel at the left

[2]

The Virgin Blachernitissa and angels. Detail: angel at the right

[2]

The Enthroned Christ and the donor

[3]

The Enthroned Christ and the donor. Detail: Christ enthroned

[3]

The Enthroned Christ and the donor.
Detail: Theodore Metochites, the donor (for color, see frontispiece of Vol. 1)

[3]

The Enthroned Christ and the donor. Detail: bust of Christ

[3]

St. Peter

[4]

St. Paul

[5]

31

St. Peter. Detail: half-figure

[4]

St. Paul. Detail: bust

[5]

St. Peter. Detail: head

[4]

St. Paul. Detail: head

[5]

The Deesis

[6]

a

b

The Deesis. Details
a. Isaac Comnenus   *b*. Melane the nun

[6]

The Deesis. Detail: the Virgin

[6]

The Deesis. Detail: Christ Chalkites

[6]

The Deesis. Detail: head of the Virgin

[6]

The Deesis. Detail: head of Christ

[6]

The southern dome. View from below

[7] – [46]

The southern dome. View from the south

[7] - [46]

Christ Pantocrator, medallion of the southern dome

[7]

The Genealogy of Christ. Noah [10] and Cainan [11]
[10], [11]

The Genealogy of Christ. Abel [31], Adam [8], and Seth [9]

[8], [9], [31]

The Genealogy of Christ. Maleleel [12] and Jared [13]

[12], [13]

The Genealogy of Christ. Lamech [14] and Sem [15]

[14], [15]

The Genealogy of Christ. Japheth [16], Arphaxad [17], and Sala [18]

[16] – [18]

The Genealogy of Christ. Heber [19], Saruch [20], and Nachor [21]

[19] – [21]

The Genealogy of Christ. Thara [22], Abraham [23], and Isaac [24]

[22] – [24]

The Genealogy of Christ. Isaac [24] and Jacob [25]

[24], [25]

54

The Genealogy of Christ. Jacob, detail

[25]

The Genealogy of Christ. Phalec [26] and Ragau [27]

[26], [27]

The Genealogy of Christ. Mathusala [28], Enoch [29], and Enos [30]

[28] - [30]

The Genealogy of Christ. Reuben [32] and Simeon [33]

[32], [33]

The Genealogy of Christ. Levi [34], Judah [35], and Zebulun [36]

[34] − [36]

The Genealogy of Christ. Zebulun [36], Issachar [37], and Dan [38]

[36] – [38]

The Genealogy of Christ. Gad [39] and Asher [40]
[39], [40]

The Genealogy of Christ. Naphtali [41] and Joseph [42]

[41], [42]

The Genealogy of Christ. Benjamin [43] and Pharez [44]

[43], [44]

The Genealogy of Christ. Zarah [45] and Esrom [46]

[45], [46]

a

b

c

d

The southern dome. Medallions of angels beneath the cornice

a. Angel at the east [47]   *b.* Angel at the west [49]

c. Angel at the south [48]   *d.* Angel at the north [50]

[47] – [50]

The northern dome. View from below

[51] – [78]

The northern dome. View from the east

[51] – [78]

The Virgin and Christ Child, medallion of the northern dome

[51]

The Virgin and Christ Child, medallion of the northern dome. Detail: head of the Virgin

[51]

The Virgin and Christ Child, medallion of the northern dome.
Detail: bust of the Christ Child

[51]

The Genealogy of Christ. Salathiel [67] and David [52]

[52], [67]

The Genealogy of Christ. Solomon [53] and Roboam [54]

[53], [54]

The Genealogy of Christ. Abia [55] and Asa [56]

[55], [56]

The Genealogy of Christ. Josaphat [57] and Joram [58]

[57], [58]

The Genealogy of Christ. Ozias [59] and Joatham [60]

[59], [60]

The Genealogy of Christ. Achaz [61] and Ezekias [62]
[61], [62]

The Genealogy of Christ. Manasses [63] and Amon [64]

[63], [64]

The Genealogy of Christ. Josias [65] and Jechonias [66]

[65], [66]

The Genealogy of Christ. Hananiah [68] and Azariah [69]

[68], [69]

The Genealogy of Christ. Mishael [70] and Daniel [71]

[70], [71]

The Genealogy of Christ. Joshua [72] and Moses [73]

[72], [73]

The Genealogy of Christ. Moses [73] and Aaron [74]

[73], [74]

a

b

The Genealogy of Christ
a. Hur [75]   *b*. Samuel [76]

[75], [76]

a   *b*

The Genealogy of Christ
a. Job [77]   *b.* Melchizedek [78]
[77], [78]

a

b

c

The northern dome. Medallions of angels beneath the cornice

a. Angel at the east [79]   b. Angel at the south [80]

c. Angel at the west [81]

[79] - [81]

Joachim's Offerings Rejected

[82]

Joachim's Offerings Rejected. Detail: Zacharias the High Priest

[82]

An unidentified scene from the life of the Virgin

[83]

An unidentified scene from the life of the Virgin. Detail

[83]

Joachim in the Wilderness

[84]

Joachim in the Wilderness. Detail: Joachim

[84]

The Annunciation to St. Anne.
Lunette, showing the position of a destroyed scene at the left

[85]

The Annunciation to St. Anne

[85]

The Annunciation to St. Anne. Detail: Anne and the angel

[85]

The Annunciation to St. Anne. Detail: the angel and the birds

[85]

The Meeting of Joachim and Anne

[86]

The Meeting of Joachim and Anne. Detail: Joachim and Anne

[86]

The Birth of the Virgin

[87]

The Birth of the Virgin. Detail: Anne and attendants

[87]

The Birth of the Virgin. Detail: preparation of the cradle

[87]

The Birth of the Virgin. Detail: preparation of the bath

[87]

The Birth of the Virgin. Detail: the midwife and the infant Mary

[87]

The Birth of the Virgin. Detail: heads of the midwife and Mary

[87]

The First Seven Steps of the Virgin

[88]

The First Seven Steps of the Virgin. Detail: the attendant, Mary, and Anne

[88]

The First Seven Steps of the Virgin. Detail: the attendant and Mary

[88]

The First Seven Steps of the Virgin. Detail: Mary

[88]

Vault of the second bay, inner narthex
Above: The Virgin Blessed by the Priests [89];
below: The Virgin Caressed by Her Parents [90]

[89], [90]

The Virgin Blessed by the Priests

[89]

The Virgin Blessed by the Priests. Detail: Joachim and Mary

[89]

The Virgin Blessed by the Priests. Detail: Joachim (half-figure) and Mary

[89]

The Virgin Blessed by the Priests. Detail: the priests

[89]

The Virgin Blessed by the Priests. Detail: the second priest

[89]

The Virgin Caressed by Her Parents

[90]

The Virgin Caressed by Her Parents. Detail: Joachim, Mary, and Anne

[90]

The Virgin Caressed by Her Parents. Detail: the southeastern quadrant of the vault

[90]

The Virgin Caressed by Her Parents. Detail: peacock in the southeastern pendentive

[90]

The Virgin Caressed by Her Parents. Detail: peacock in the northeastern pendentive

[90]

Vault of the third bay, inner narthex. The Presentation of the Virgin in the Temple

[91]

The Presentation of the Virgin in the Temple. Eastern half

[91]

The Presentation of the Virgin in the Temple. Western half

[91]

The Presentation of the Virgin in the Temple. Detail: the Holy of Holies

[91]

The Presentation of the Virgin in the Temple. Detail: two attendants

[91]

The Presentation of the Virgin in the Temple. Detail: two attendants

[91]

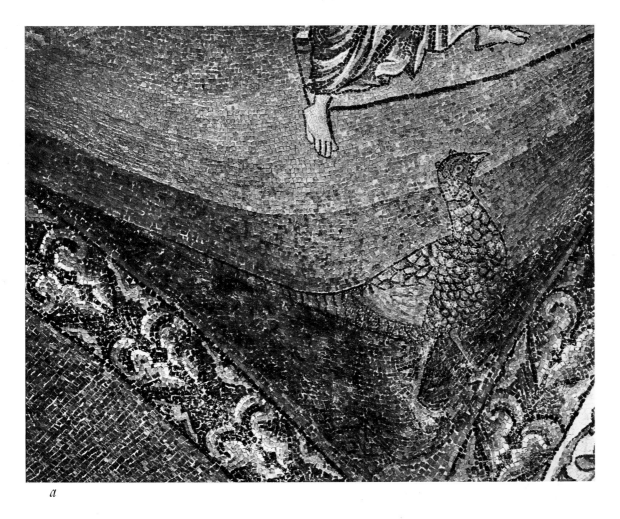

a

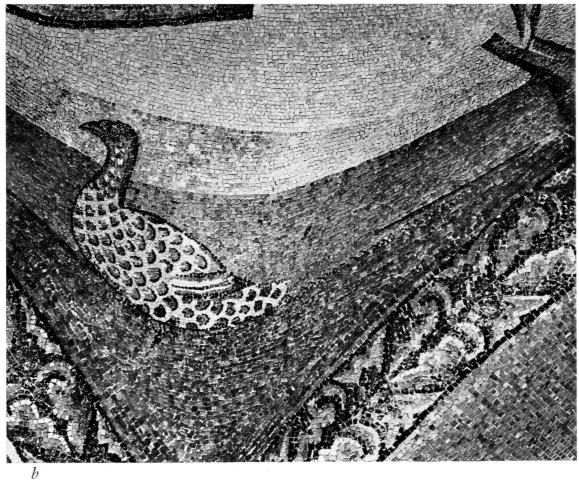

b

The Presentation of the Virgin in the Temple. Details
a. Male pheasant, in the northeastern pendentive
b. Female pheasant, in the southeastern pendentive

[91]

The Virgin Fed by an Angel

[92]

The Virgin Fed by an Angel. Detail: Mary, the angel, and the attendant

[92]

The Virgin Fed by an Angel. Detail: the attendant

[92]

Instruction of the Virgin in the Temple

[93]

The Virgin Receiving the Skein of Purple Wool. Detail: priests and architecture

[94]

The Virgin Receiving the Skein of Purple Wool

[94]

The Virgin Receiving the Skein of Purple Wool. Detail: the priests

[94]

The Virgin Receiving the Skein of Purple Wool.
Detail: Mary and a virgin of the tribe of David

[94]

The Virgin Receiving the Skein of Purple Wool. Detail: virgins of the tribe of David

[94]

Zacharias Praying before the Rods of the Suitors

[95]

Zacharias Praying before the Rods of the Suitors. Detail: the Holy of Holies

[95]

Zacharias Praying before the Rods of the Suitors. Detail: Zacharias

[95]

Η ΠΡΟΣ ΤΟΝ ΙΩΣΗΦ ΠΑΡΑΔΟCIC

The Virgin Entrusted to Joseph

[96]

The Virgin Entrusted to Joseph. Detail: the rejected suitors (half-figures)

[96]

The Virgin Entrusted to Joseph. Detail: Zacharias and Mary

[96]

The Virgin Entrusted to Joseph. Detail: the rejected suitors

[96]

The Virgin Entrusted to Joseph. Detail: Zacharias and Mary before the Holy of Holies

[96]

Joseph Taking the Virgin to His House

[97]

Joseph Taking the Virgin to His House. Detail: Mary, Joseph, and a son of Joseph

[97]

Joseph Taking the Virgin to His House. Detail: Joseph and his son

[97]

The Annunciation to the Virgin at the Well

[98]

The Annunciation to the Virgin at the Well. Detail: Mary and the angel

[98]

Joseph Taking Leave of the Virgin; Joseph Reproaching the Virgin

[99]

148

Joseph Taking Leave of the Virgin. Detail: Mary and Joseph

[99]

Joseph Taking Leave of the Virgin. Detail: a son of Joseph

[99]

Joseph Reproaching the Virgin

[99]

Joseph Dreaming; The Virgin and Two Companions; The Journey to Bethlehem

[100]

152

Joseph Dreaming; The Virgin and Two Companions. Detail

[100]

The Virgin and Two Companions. Detail

[100]

The Journey to Bethlehem. Detail: Joseph, Mary, and a son of Joseph

The Journey to Bethlehem. Detail: Joseph

[100]

The Journey to Bethlehem. Detail: Mary on the donkey

[100]

The Journey to Bethlehem. Detail: a son of Joseph

[100]

The Enrollment for Taxation

[101]

The Enrollment for Taxation. Detail: Cyrenius and a guard

[101]

The Enrollment for Taxation. Detail: the scribe, the officer, and Mary

[101]

The Enrollment for Taxation. Detail: head of Cyrenius

[101]

The Enrollment for Taxation. Detail: Mary, Joseph, and the four sons of Joseph

[101]

The Enrollment for Taxation. Detail: heads of the scribe and the officer

[101]

The Enrollment for Taxation. Detail: heads of Joseph and his sons

[101]

The Nativity

[102]

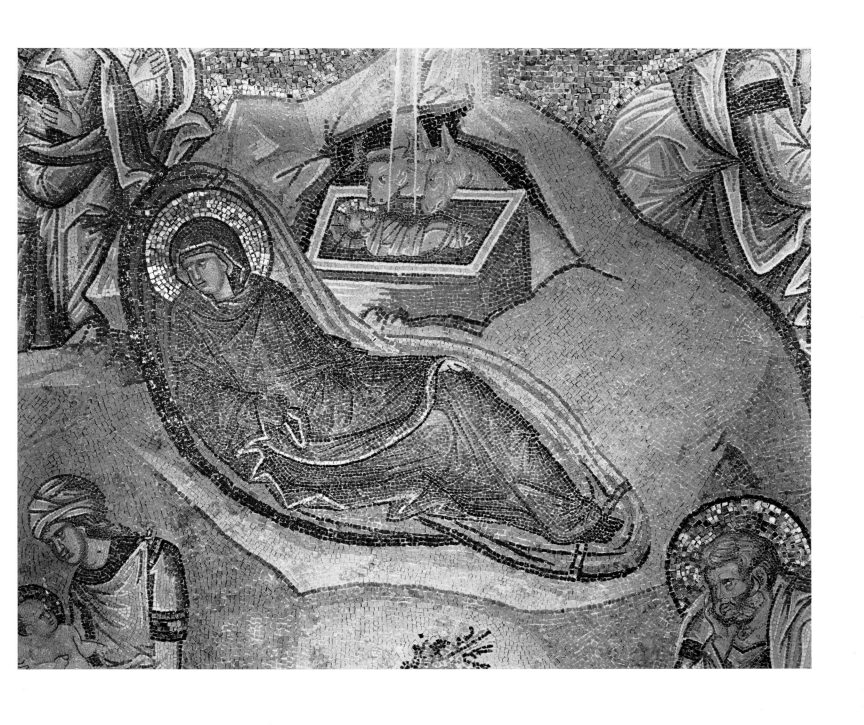

The Nativity. Detail: Mary before the cave and the manger

[102]

The Nativity. Detail: the heralding angels

[102]

The Nativity. Detail: preparation of the bath

[102]

The Nativity. Detail: the Child in the manger, the ox, and the ass

[102]

The Nativity. Detail: Joseph

The Nativity. Detail: the annunciation to the shepherds

[102]

The Journey of the Magi; The Magi before Herod

[103]

The Magi before Herod. Detail: the Magi

[103]

The Magi before Herod. Detail: Herod and his guard

[103]

The Journey of the Magi. Detail

[103]

Herod Inquiring of the Priests and Scribes

[104]

Herod Inquiring of the Priests and Scribes. Detail: Herod

[104]

Herod Inquiring of the Priests and Scribes. Detail: the guard

[104]

a

b

Two lunettes of the seventh bay, outer narthex, showing the positions of lost mosaics
a. Northern lunette (the position of the Adoration of the Magi?)
b. Eastern lunette: The Return of the Magi to the East [105]

[105]

The Return of the Magi to the East. Detail

[105]

The Flight into Egypt
Left: The Flight; *right:* The Idols Falling from the Walls of the Temple

[106]

The Flight into Egypt. Detail: the Idols Falling from the Walls of the Temple

[106]

Herod Ordering the Massacre of the Innocents

[107]

Herod Ordering the Massacre of the Innocents. Detail: Herod and soldiers

[107]

Herod Ordering the Massacre of the Innocents. Detail: a mother

[107]

Herod Ordering the Massacre of the Innocents. Detail: soldiers

[107]

Herod Ordering the Massacre of the Innocents. Detail: a soldier in pursuit

[107]

Herod Ordering the Massacre of the Innocents. Detail: a mother seeking to hide

[107]

The Massacre of the Innocents

[108]

The Massacre of the Innocents. Detail from the left fragment

[108]

The Massacre of the Innocents. Detail from the left fragment

[108]

The Massacre of the Innocents. The right fragment

[108]

The Mothers Mourning Their Children

[109]

The Mothers Mourning Their Children. Detail

[109]

The Mothers Mourning Their Children. Detail: a group of the mothers

[109]

The Flight of Elizabeth and John

[110]

The Flight of Elizabeth and John. Detail: a soldier

[110]

The Flight of Elizabeth and John. Detail: Elizabeth and John in the mountain

[110]

Joseph Dreaming; The Return of the Holy Family from Egypt

[111]

Joseph Dreaming. Detail

[111]

The Return of the Holy Family from Egypt. Detail: the donkey and a son of Joseph

[111]

The Return of the Holy Family from Egypt. Detail: Nazareth

[111]

The Return of the Holy Family from Egypt. Detail: the Holy Family

[111]

The Return of the Holy Family from Egypt. Detail: the Holy Family

[111]

Christ Taken to Jerusalem for Passover

[112]

Christ Taken to Jerusalem for Passover. Detail: Jerusalem

[112]

Christ Taken to Jerusalem for Passover. Detail: the Holy Family

[112]

Christ Taken to Jerusalem for Passover. Detail: Christ and two sons of Joseph

[112]

Christ Taken to Jerusalem for Passover. Detail: Joseph

[112]

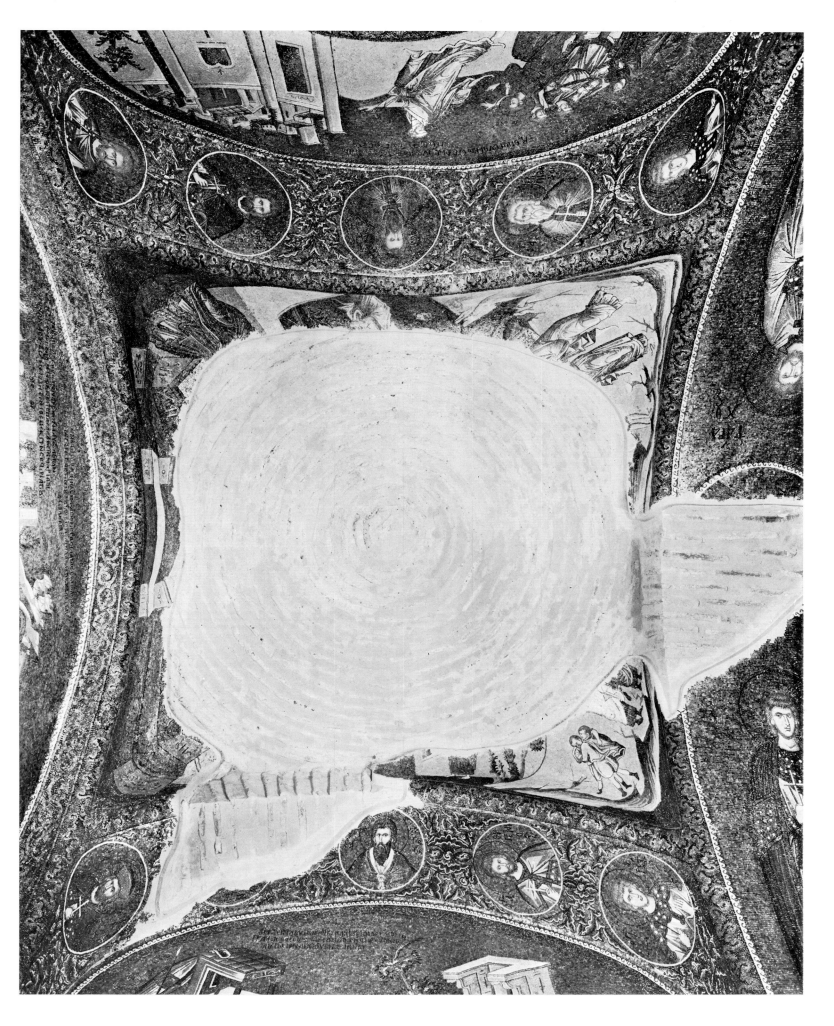

Vault of the first bay, outer narthex

In domical vault: *left*, [113]; *right*, [114]. Medallions in arches: *above*, [147] - [151];
below, [142] - [146]; *right*, [152]. Figures in right arch: [154] and [153]

[113], [114], [142] - [154]

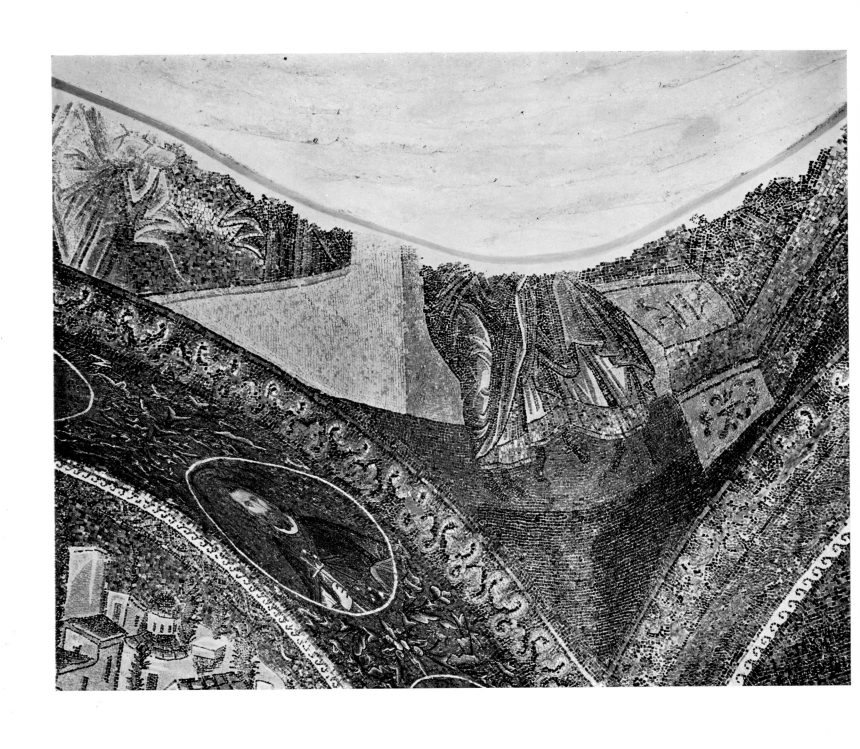

Christ among the Doctors. Detail, fragment in the northwestern pendentive

[113]

Christ among the Doctors. Detail, fragment in the northeastern pendentive

[113]

Left: Christ among the Doctors [113]. Detail: Christ Tarrying in Jerusalem?
Right: John the Baptist Bearing Witness of Christ (I) [114]. Detail
Fragment in the southeastern pendentive

[113], [114]

John the Baptist Bearing Witness of Christ (I).
Detail, fragment in the southwestern pendentive

[114]

Vault of the second bay, outer narthex

In domical vault: *left*, [115]; *right*, [116].

Medallions in arches: *above*, [160] - [164]; *below*, [155] - [159]; *left*, [152].

Figures in arches: *left*, [154] and [153]; *right*, [167] and [165]

[115], [116], [152] - [165], [167]

John the Baptist Bearing Witness of Christ (II)

[115]

John the Baptist Bearing Witness of Christ (II). Detail: the priests and Levites

[115]

John the Baptist Bearing Witness of Christ (II).
Detail: John the Baptist, Christ, and the disciples John and Andrew

[115]

John the Baptist Bearing Witness of Christ (II). Detail: John the Baptist and Christ

[115]

John the Baptist Bearing Witness of Christ (II). Detail: the disciples John and Andrew

[115]

The Temptation of Christ

[116]

The Temptation of Christ. Detail: the stones and the kingdoms

[116]

The Temptation of Christ. Detail: the high mountain and the pinnacle of the temple

[116]

The Temptation of Christ. Detail: the high mountain

[116]

The Temptation of Christ. Detail: the kingdoms

[116]

The Temptation of Christ. Detail: the devil

[116]

Vault of the third bay, outer narthex
In domical vault: *left*, [117]; *right*, [118].
Figures in arches: *left*, [167] and [165]; *right*, [168] and [166]

[117], [118], [165] - [168]

The Miracle at Cana

[117]

The Miracle at Cana. Detail, fragment in the northwestern pendentive

[117]

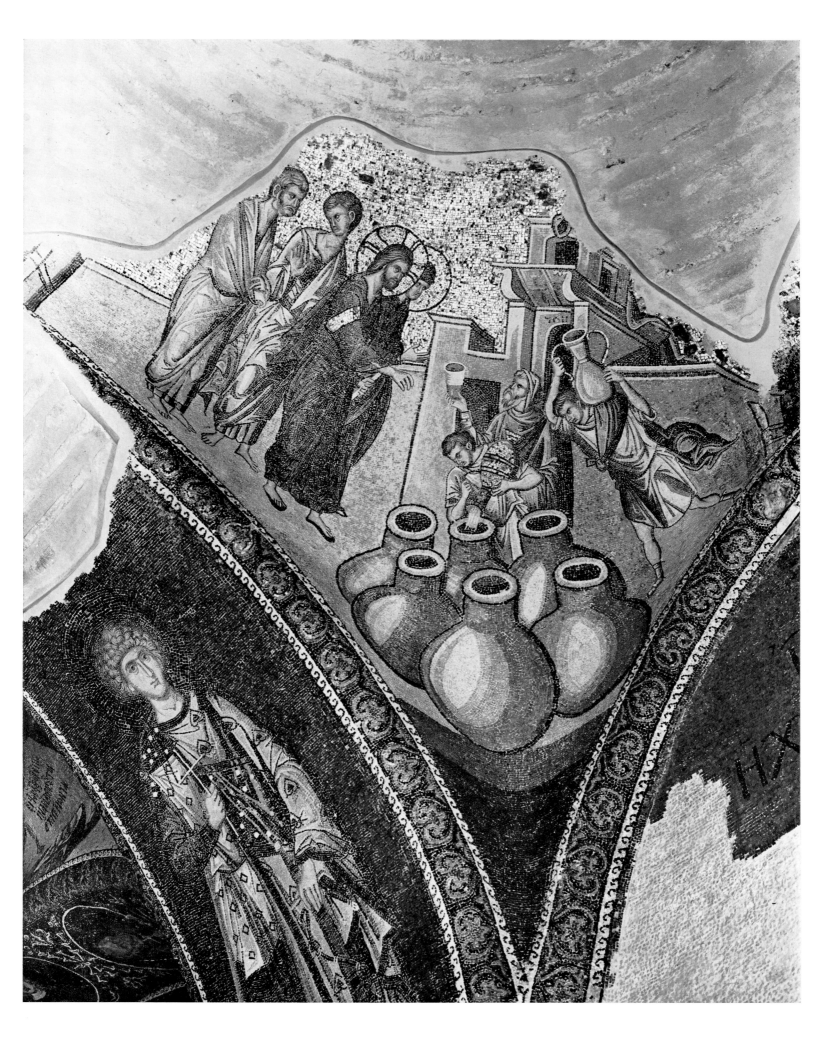

The Miracle at Cana. Detail, fragment in the northeastern pendentive

[117]

The Miracle at Cana. Detail: the marriage feast

[117]

The Miracle at Cana. Detail: the slaying of a bullock

[117]

The Miracle at Cana. Detail: two disciples, Christ, and Mary

[117]

The Miracle at Cana. Detail: pouring water into jars

[117]

The Miracle at Cana. Detail: the servants and the governor of the feast

[117]

The Miracle at Cana. Detail: ornament above the door of the building at the far right

[117]

The Multiplication of Loaves

[118]

The Multiplication of Loaves. Detail, fragment in the southeastern pendentive

[118]

The Multiplication of Loaves. Detail: Christ giving thanks

[118]

The Multiplication of Loaves. Detail: Christ giving bread to two disciples

[118]

The Multiplication of Loaves. Detail: a company of the multitude

[118]

The Multiplication of Loaves. Detail: a group of children

[118]

The Multiplication of Loaves.
Detail: the twelve baskets, fragment in the southwestern pendentive

[118]

244

The Multiplication of Loaves. Detail: a second company of the multitude

[118]

Vault of the fourth bay, outer narthex

In domical vault: *above*, [120]; *below*, [119]. Medallions in arches: *above*, [172] - [174];
below, [169] - [171]. Figures in arches: *left*, [168] and [166]; *right*, [176] and [175]

[119], [120], [166], [168] - [176]

Christ Healing a Leper

[119]

Above: an unidentified scene [120]; *below:* [110]

[110], [120]

Vault of the fifth bay, outer narthex

Medallions in arches: *above*, [178]; *below*, [177]. Figures in arch at left:
above, [176]; *below*, [175]

[175] – [178]

Vault of the sixth bay, outer narthex

[121] – [129]

a

b

Two scenes in the northeastern pendentive of the sixth bay

a. Left: Christ Healing the Paralytic at the Pool of Bethesda, [121] above and inscription
of [128] below; *right:* an unidentified scene [122]   *b.* Christ Healing the Paralytic at the
Pool of Bethesda: second episode, the paralytic healed [128]

[121], [122], [128]

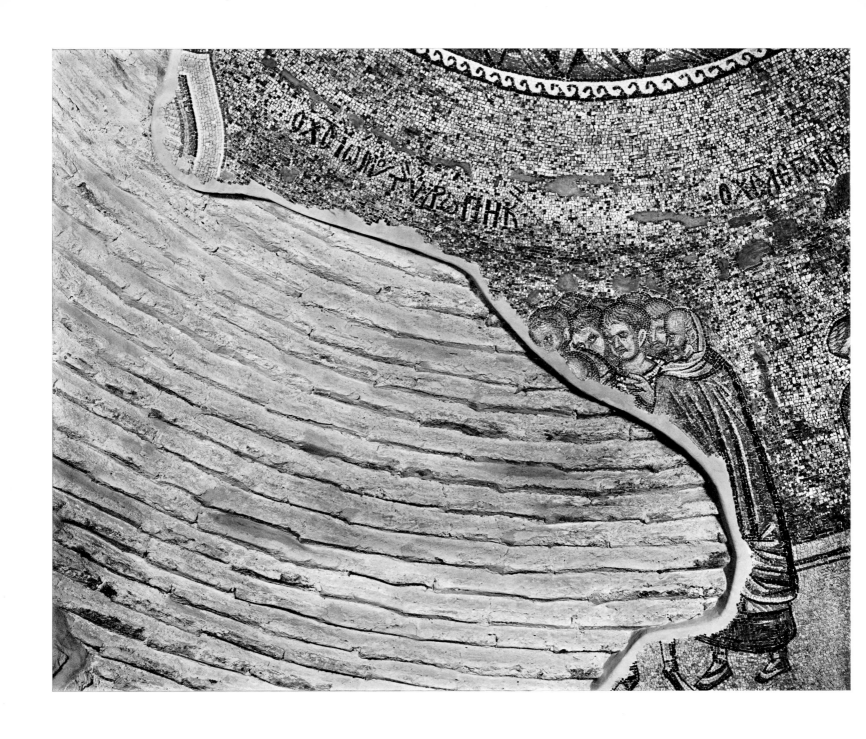

Upper left: an unidentified scene [122]; *center*, Christ Healing the Dropsical Man [123];
upper right, inscription of [124]

[122] – [124]

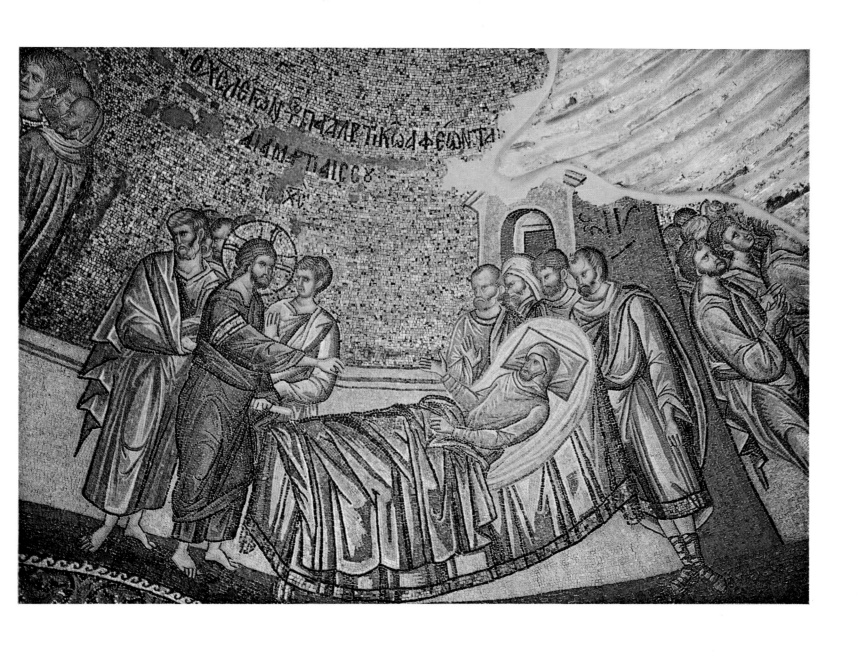

Christ Healing the Paralytic at Capernaum

[124]

Christ Healing the Paralytic at Capernaum. Detail: Christ and four disciples

[124]

Christ Healing the Paralytic at Capernaum. Detail: the paralytic and his bearers

[124]

An unidentified scene. Detail: a group of disciples

[125]

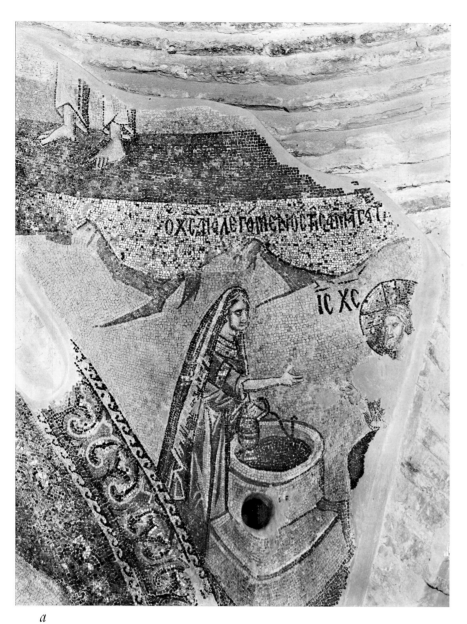

a

b

Scenes in the northwestern and southeastern pendentives of the sixth bay
a. The northwestern pendentive: *above*, an unidentified scene [126]; *below*, Christ and
the Samaritan Woman at the Well [127]
b. The southeastern pendentive: Christ Healing the Blind Born (?) [129]

[126], [127], [129]

Vault of the seventh bay, outer narthex

[130] - [133]

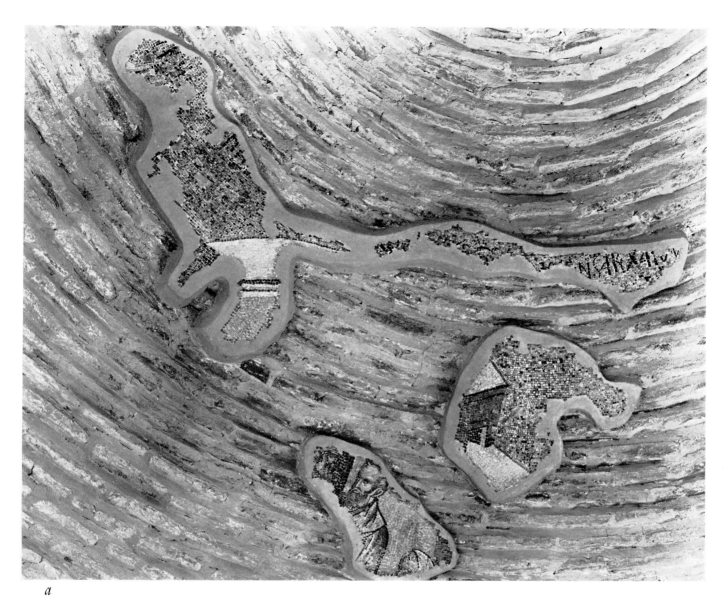

a

b

Scenes in the vault of the seventh bay
a. Upper left: fragmentary inscription of [130]; *center:* an unidentified scene [131];
upper right: fragmentary inscription of [132]
b. Left: Christ Calling Zacchaeus [132]; *right:* an unidentified scene [133]

[130] – [133]

Christ Healing a Blind and Dumb Man

[134]

Christ Healing a Blind and Dumb Man. Detail: the blind and dumb man, Peter, and Christ

[134]

Christ Healing Two Blind Men

[135]

Christ Healing Two Blind Men. Detail: the blind men

[135]

Christ Healing Peter's Mother-in-Law

[136]

Christ Healing Peter's Mother-in-Law. Detail: John and Andrew

[136]

Christ Healing Peter's Mother-in-Law. Detail: Christ, Peter, and Peter's mother-in-law

[136]

Christ Healing Peter's Mother-in-Law. Detail: head of Peter

[136]

Christ Healing the Woman with the Issue of Blood

[137]

Christ Healing the Woman with the Issue of Blood. Detail: Peter, John, and Christ

[137]

Christ Healing the Woman with the Issue of Blood. Detail: the woman

[137]

Christ Healing the Woman with the Issue of Blood. Detail: Jairus and others

[137]

Christ Healing the Man with the Withered Hand

[138]

Christ Healing the Man with the Withered Hand. Detail

[138]

Christ Healing the Leper

[139]

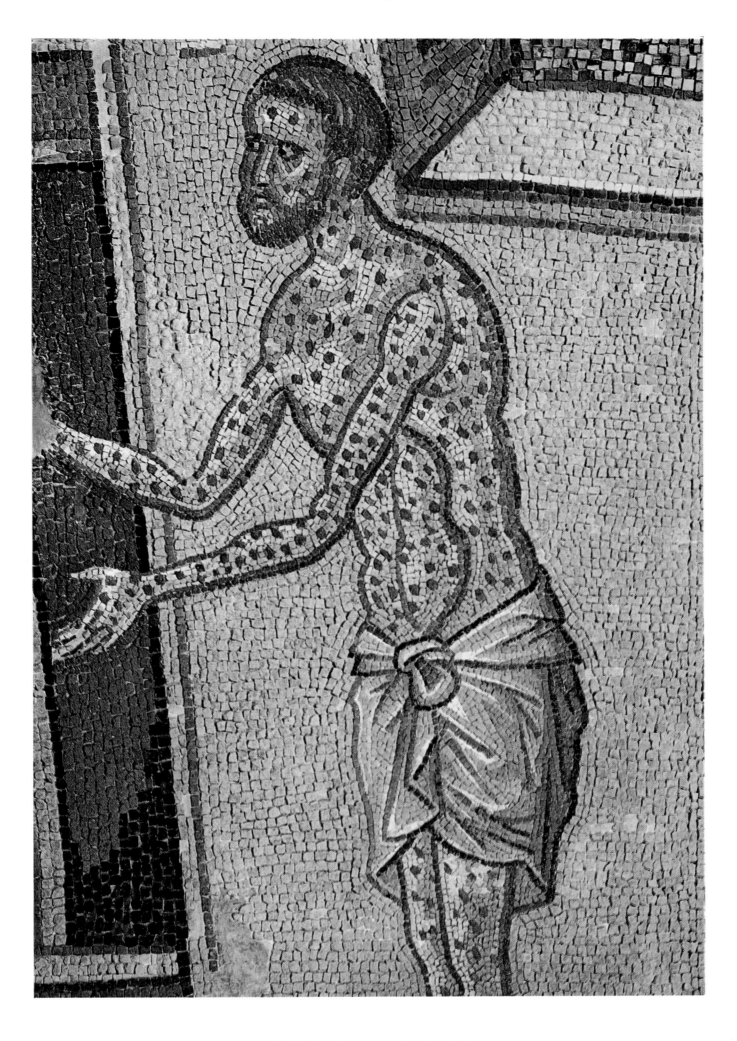

Christ Healing the Leper. Detail: the leper

[139]

An unidentified scene (a miracle of healing)

[140]

Christ Healing a Multitude

[141]

Christ Healing a Multitude. Detail: disciples

[141]

Christ Healing a Multitude. Detail: Christ and a group of the afflicted, center

[141]

Christ Healing a Multitude. Detail: a group of the afflicted, center

[141]

Christ Healing a Multitude. Detail: a group of the afflicted, right

[141]

a

b

c

d

Medallion portraits in the arches of the outer narthex, first and second bays

a. First bay, eastern arch [142] - [146]   *b.* First bay, western arch [147] - [151]
c. Second bay, eastern arch [155] - [159]   *d.* Second bay, western arch [160] - [164]

[142] - [151], [155] - [164]

a

b

c

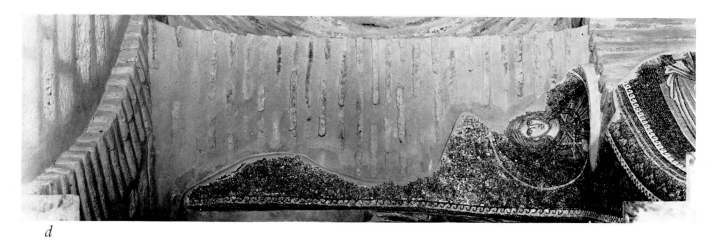

d

Medallion portraits in the arches of the outer narthex, fourth and fifth bays

a. Fourth bay, eastern arch [169] - [171]   b. Fourth bay, western arch [172] - [174]
c. Fifth bay, eastern arch [177]   d. Fifth bay, western arch [178]

[169] - [174], [177], [178]

St. Mardarius

[142]

St. Auxentius

[143]

St. Eustratius

[144]

St. Eugenius

[145]

St. Orestes

[146]

St. Anempodistus

[147]

ϹΓ ελ
ΟΔ ΠΙΔΗ
    ΦΟϹ

St. Elpidephorus

[148]

St. Acindynus

[149]

St. Aphthonius

[150]

St. Pegasius

[151]

St. Andronicus

[153]

St. Tarachus

[154]

St. Philemon

[155]

St. Leucius

[156]

St. Agathonicus

[157]

St. Thyrsus

[158]

St. Apollonius

[159]

a

b

a. St. Laurus [160]   *b.* St. Florus [161]

[160], [161]

a

b

a. St. Menas of Phrygia [162]   *b.* St. Victor [163]
[162], [163]

St. Vincentius

[164]

St. George (?)

[165]

St. Demetrius (?)

[166]

a

b

a. An unidentified saint [167]   *b*. An unidentified saint [168]

[167], [168]

a

b

a. St. Abibus [169]   *b.* St. Samonas [171]

[169], [171]

St. Gurias

[170]

a

b

a. St. Eugraphus [172] *b.* St. Menas of Alexandria [173]

[172], [173]

St. Hermogenes

[174]

An unidentified saint

[175]

An unidentified saint

[176]

a

b

a. An unidentified saint [177] *b.* St. Sergius or St. Bacchus [178]

[177], [178]

St. Anne and the Infant Mary

[179]

St. Joachim (?)

[180]

The Virgin and Child (Hodegetria)

[181]

St. John the Baptist

[182]

An unidentified military saint

[183]

St. Euthymius

[184]

The Dormition of the Virgin

[185]

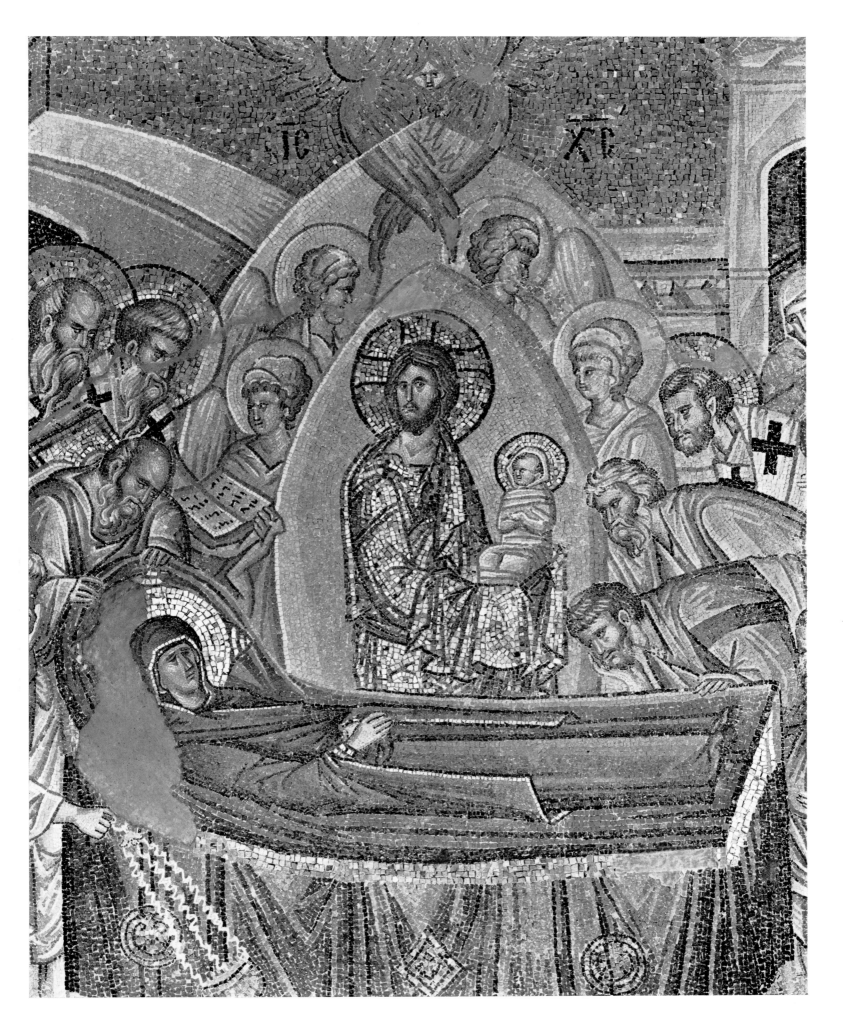

The Dormition of the Virgin.
Detail: the Virgin, and Christ in glory receiving the soul of the Virgin

[185]

The Dormition of the Virgin. Detail: a group of apostles and bishops, left

[185]

The Dormition of the Virgin. Detail: a group of apostles, a bishop, and women, right

[185]

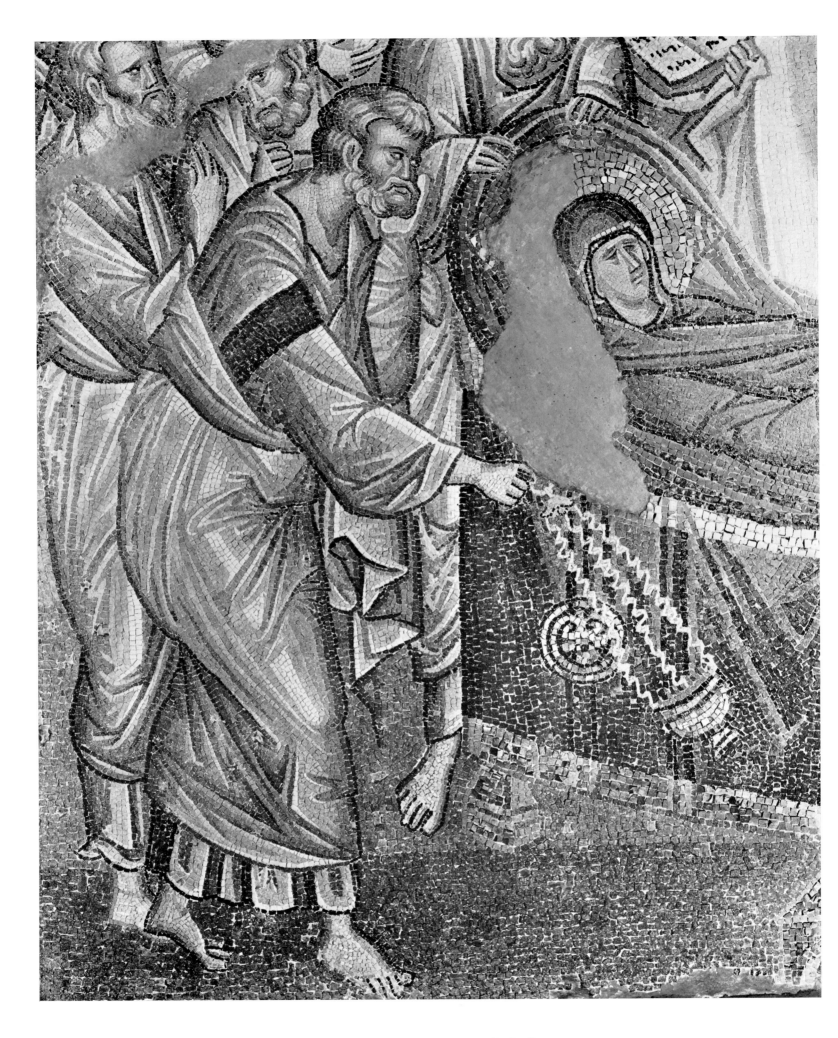

The Dormition of the Virgin. Detail: St. Peter

[185]

The Dormition of the Virgin. Detail: Christ receiving the soul of the Virgin

[185]

The Dormition of the Virgin. Detail: bust of St. Peter

[185]

The Dormition of the Virgin. Detail: women in the doorway

[185]

The templon mosaics. Christ

[186]

The templon mosaics. The Virgin Hodegetria

[187]

The Virgin Hodegetria. Detail

[187]

ORNAMENTS

a

b

c

Ornamental medallions in the centers of the domical vaults
a. Inner narthex, second bay   *b*. Outer narthex, second bay
c. Outer narthex, sixth bay. Detail

a

b

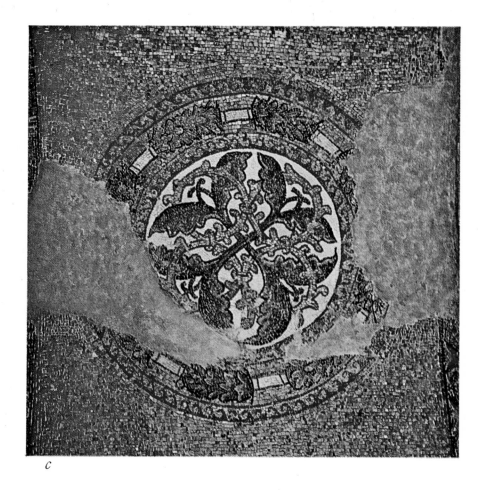

c

Ornamental medallions in the transverse arches of the inner narthex
a. Arch between the first and second bays   *b.* Arch between the third and fourth bays
c. Arch between the second and third bays

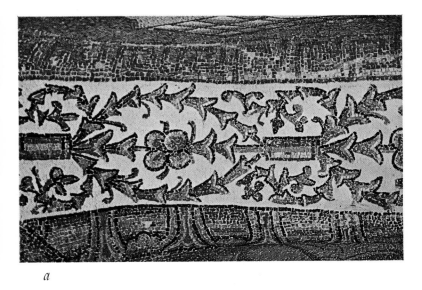

a

b

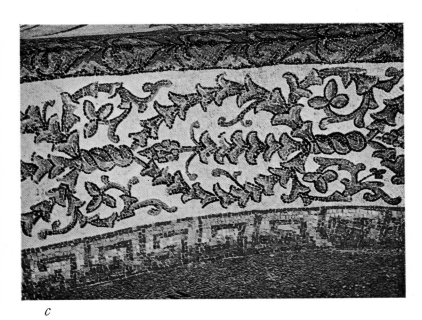

c

d

Floral ornaments in the eastern and western arches of the inner narthex
a. Second bay, eastern arch *b*. Second bay, western arch
c. Third bay, eastern arch *d*. Third bay, western arch

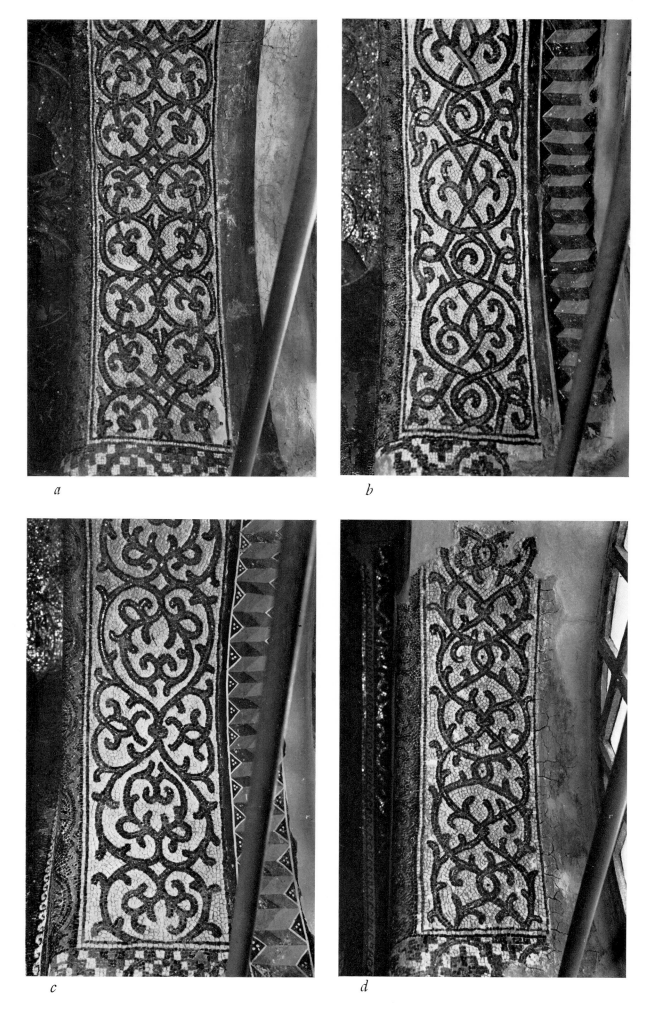

Specimens of ornamental motifs in the window soffits of the outer narthex

a. Window of first bay   *b.* Window of second bay
c. Window of fourth bay   *d.* Window of sixth bay

Iconographic Index

Iconographic Index

Bracketed numbers are those assigned to the mosaic and fresco subjects, in an order corresponding with the iconographic sequence of the subjects in the church; the same order is followed in the present volumes. Numbers not in brackets refer to the plates in Vols. 2 and 3. PL. 1–334 (mosaics) are in Vol. 2, PL. 335–553 (frescoes and tombs) in Vol. 3.

Aaron [74], 82
  and His Sons before Altar [236], 466–468
Abel [31], 46
Abia [55], 73
Abibus, St. [169], 283 *a*, 307 *a*
Abraham [23], 53
  in Paradise, *see* Lazarus the Beggar (Last Judgment)
Achaz [61], 76
Acindynus, St. [149], 282 *b*, 291
Adam [8], 46, 47
Agathonicus, St. [157], 282 *c*, 298
Amnos, in prothesis, conch of apse, 524
Amon [64], 77
Anastasis [201], 341–359
Andrew, St., in dome of diaconicon, 526
Andronicus, St. [153], 294
Anempodistus, St. [147], 282 *b*, 289
Angel and Soul (Last Judgment) [206], 393
Angel Smiting Assyrians before Jerusalem [235], 461, 464, 465
Angels and archangels:
  attending Christ, Tomb C, 536 *b* and *c*
  attending Virgin, [2], 20, 24, 25; [210], 407; [212]–[223], 409, 410, 412–425
  in Divine Liturgy, in dome of prothesis, 521–523
  in medallions, [47]–[50], 65; [79]–[81], 85
  Michael, Archangel, medallion [242], 472, 473
  See also Last Judgment
Anne, St.:
  and Joachim meeting [86], 96, 97
  annunciation to [85], 92–95
  with infant Mary [179], 314
Annunciation:
  to St. Anne [85], 92–95
  to Virgin at Well [98], 146, 147
Aphthonius, St. [150], 282 *b*, 292
Apollonius, St. [159], 282 *c*, 300
Apostles:
  in dome of diaconicon, 525–528
  in Last Judgment [204]–2, 376–379, 381–383
  See also Dormition; *and under individual names*
Ark of Covenant:
  borne to Solomon's Temple [231], 454, 455
  installation in Solomon's Temple [234], 460
Arphaxad [17], 51
Artemius, St. (?) [264], 514, 515
Asa [56], 73
Asher [40], 61
Athanasia the Nun, *see* Irene Raoulaina Palaeologina

Athanasius, St. [244], 477
Auxentius, St. [143], 282 *a*, 285
Azariah [69], 79

Bacchus, St., [178] (?), 283 *d*, 313 *b*; [265], 516
Basil, St. [246], 479, 483
Benjamin [43], 63
Betrothal of Mary and Joseph, *see* Virgin Mary, Entrusted to Joseph; Zacharias Praying before Rods of Suitors
Birth of Virgin [87], 98–103
Blachernitissa (Virgin) [2], 20–23

Cainan [11], 48
Cana, Miracle at [117], 229–237
Chalkites, *see* Deesis
Choirs of Elect (Last Judgment) [204]–3, 384, 385
Christ:
  busts of, [240], 471 *b*; [241], 471 *c*; Tomb C, 536 *a*; Tomb H, 552; *see also* Pantocrator
  among Doctors [113], 212–214
  Cursing Fig Tree (?) [130], 259 *a* (upper left)
  figures of, [3], 26, 27, 29; [186], 328; *see also* Deesis
  Healing miracles, *see under* Healing
  Reading in Synagogue (?) [131], 259 *a*
  Taken to Jerusalem for Passover [112], 206–210
  Tarrying in Jerusalem (?) [113], 214
  For other scenes of Christ's life, see individual subjects
Church Fathers, *see* Fathers *and under individual names*
Cosmas (of Maiuma), St., hymnographer [225], 428, 429, 435, 436 *b*; Tomb E, 544
Cyril (of Alexandria), St. [248], 481, 485

Dan [38], 60
Daniel [71], 80
David [52], 71
David of Thessalonike, St. [260], 506, 507
Death of Virgin, *see* Dormition
Deesis [6], 36–41
  in Last Judgment [204]–2, 373–375
Demetrius, St., [166] (?), 305; [253], 492, 493
Demetrius Doukas [Angelos Comnenos Palaeologos?], Tomb H, 551
Descent into Limbo, *see* Anastasis
Divine Liturgy, in dome of prothesis, 521–523
Dormition of Virgin [185], 320–327

Egypt:
  Flight into [106], 182, 183
  Return of Holy Family from [111], 200, 202–205

Plans and Sections

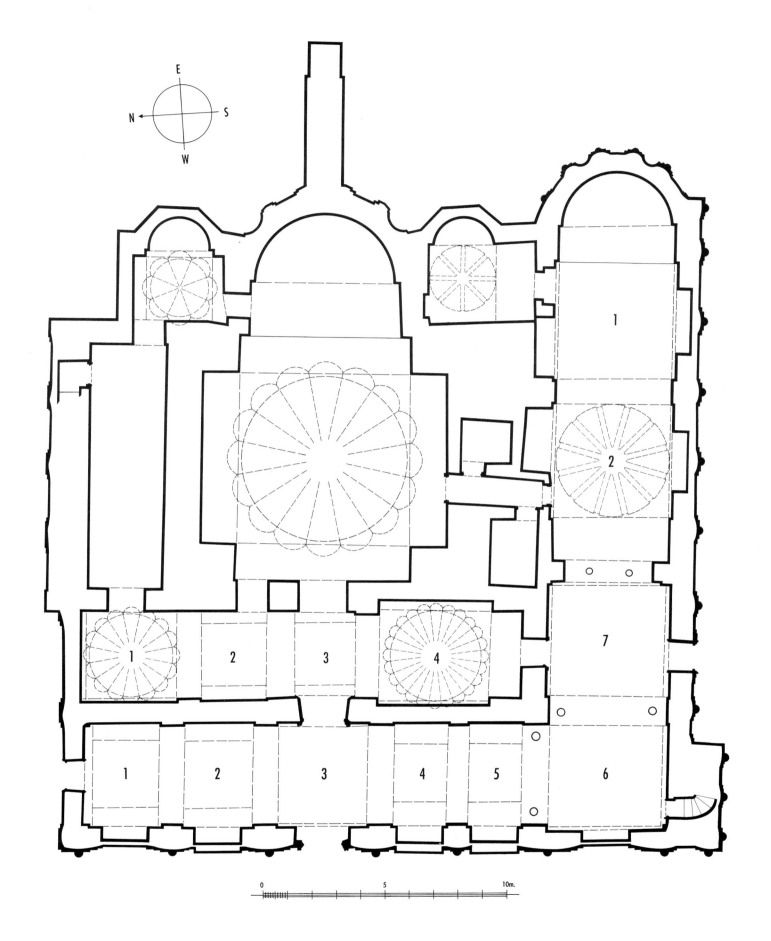

Fig. 1. General plan of the Kariye Djami

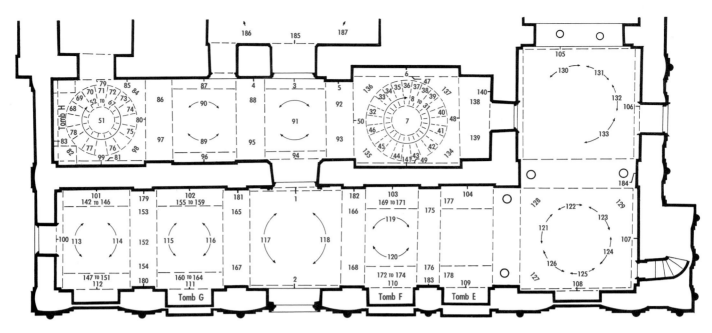

Fig. 2. Plan of the outer and inner narthexes

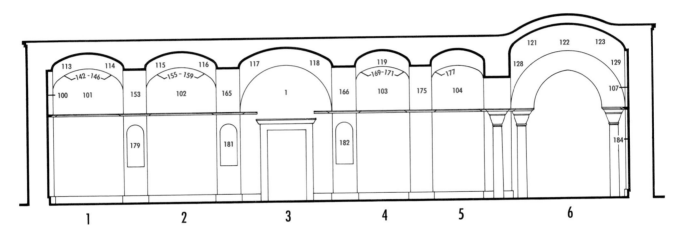

Fig. 3. Section of outer narthex, Bays 1–6, looking east

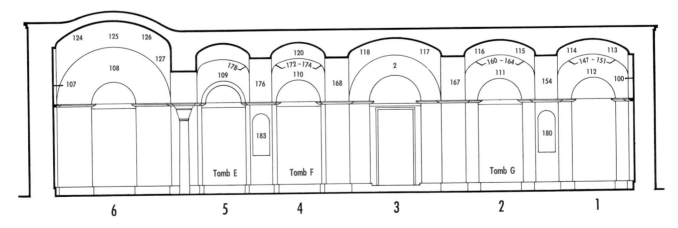

Fig. 4. Section of outer narthex, Bays 1–6, looking west

THE NARTHEXES

Key numbers in red indicate location of mosaics

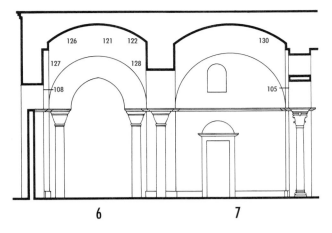

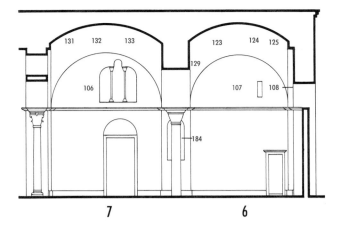

Fig. 5. Section of outer narthex, Bays 6 and 7,
looking north

Fig. 6. Section of outer narthex, Bays 6 and 7,
looking south

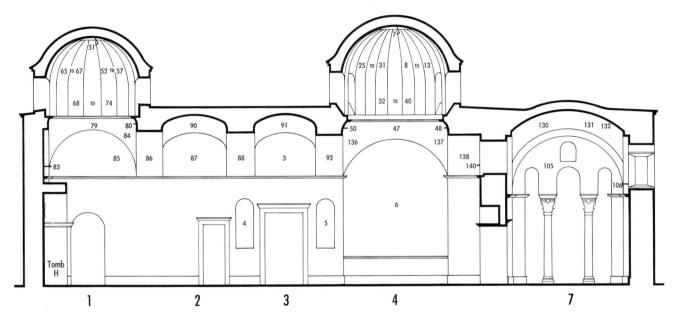

Fig. 7. Section of inner narthex, Bays 1–4, and of outer narthex, Bay 7, looking east

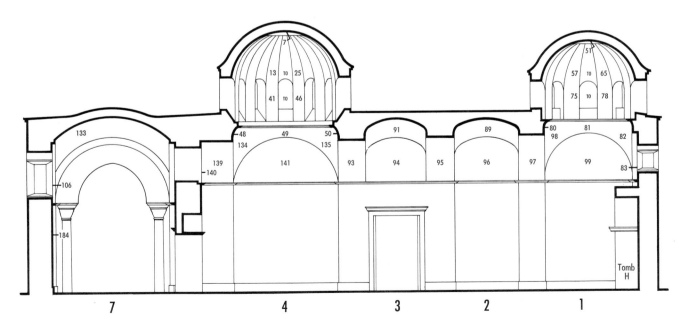

Fig. 8. Section of inner narthex, Bays 1–4, and of outer narthex, Bay 7, looking west

THE NARTHEXES

Key numbers in red indicate location of mosaics

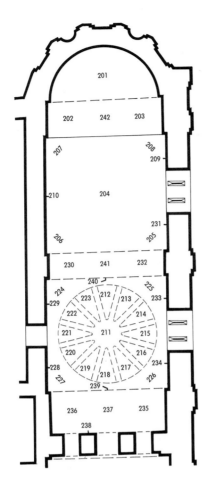

Fig. 9. Plan of the upper zone

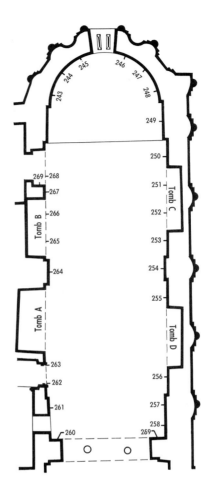

Fig. 10. Plan of the lower zone

THE PARECCLESION

Key numbers in red indicate location of frescoes

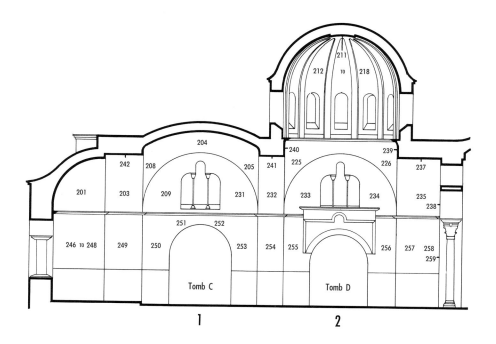

Fig. 11. Section, looking south

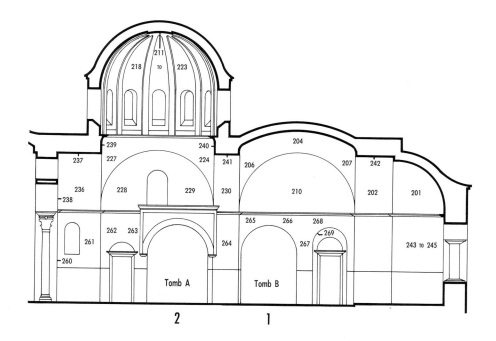

Fig. 12. Section, looking north

THE PARECCLESION

Key numbers in red indicate location of frescoes

THE ENGRAVINGS WERE MADE BY WALKER ENGRAVING CORPORATION, NEW YORK, AND PRINTED BY DAVIS, DELANEY, INC., NEW YORK.

The color plates in these volumes were reproduced from Ektachrome and Kodachrome transparencies taken over many years and under difficult conditions. The publishers wish to express their gratitude to the staff of Walker Engraving Corporation for the exceptional care and attention they devoted to manufacturing the engravings and making many subsequent corrections, and to the staff of Davis, Delaney, Inc. for their painstaking control of the presswork.

THE CAPTIONS WERE COMPOSED BY BAXTER & SPENCER, INC., NEW YORK. KINGSPORT PRESS, INC., KINGSPORT, TENNESSEE, COMPOSED AND PRINTED THE FRONT AND END MATTERS AND BOUND THE VOLUME.